Ingredients
for a
Heartfelt
Thanksgiving

from the Kids at Boys Town

D1287298

Ingredients for a Heartfelt Thanksgiving
from the Kids at Boys Town

Val J. Peter

BOYS TOWN PRESS

BOYS TOWN, NEBRASKA

Ingredients for a
Heartfelt Thanksgiving

Published by the Boys Town Press
Father Flanagan's Boys' Home
Boys Town, Nebraska 68010
www.girlsandboystown.org

© 2000 Father Flanagan's Boys' Home

All rights reserved. No part of this book may
be reproduced or transmitted in any form or by
any means, electronic or mechanical, including
photocopying, recording, or by any information
storage and retrieval system, without the written
permission of Boys Town, except where permitted
by law. For information, address Boys Town Press,
Father Flanagan's Boys' Home, 14100 Crawford St.,
Boys Town, NE 68010.

ISBN 1-889322-38-5

10   9   8   7   6   5   4   3   2   1

Table of Contents

Note: *Boys Town is a family, and like every family, we cherish our children's privacy. In this book, our children share their thoughts with you, but their names have been changed to protect their privacy.*

CHAPTER 1

Thanksgiving: A Personal Response

"Earth's crammed with heaven and every common bush afire with God."

Those words by Elizabeth Barrett Browning aptly describe the magnificent splendor of the fall foliage that is all around us as we approach the Thanksgiving season.

Here at Boys Town we give our boys and girls the opportunity to reflect on the reasons they have to be grateful. Life has failed so many of our kids – not at the end, not at the middle, but at the very beginning.

And yet, there are gifts and blessings. In the midst of our troubles, "Earth's crammed with heaven and every common bush afire with God." We structure the opportunities for our kids to say, "Thank you." It is very important for them and for your children, too. Why? Because it is gratitude that helps us hold hands together as a family. And, as the song says, "If we hold on together, I know our dreams will never die."

So take some time in the holiday season. Some night at dinner, make it a special time. Let everyone know in advance that tonight is the night that we are going to tell each other what we are thankful for. Dad or Mom, you need to take the lead. Get quiet; be sure there is enough time, and start out by telling your children what you are grateful for in their lives and in your own. Make it simple. Open your heart. Then go around the table and have each one of your children do the same.

Little children do this easily. Adolescents may find it difficult to find appropriate words. Be patient with them. Encourage them. Wait for them until they find the words. You won't regret it.

You might want to repeat it on Thanksgiving Day. Be sure you take time. Be sure you tell everyone in advance you are going to do it. Be sure it is genuine and sincere.

Each of us has many things to be grateful for, if we only open our hearts to the good that surrounds us. Please smile today and make the sun shine in your life.

CHAPTER 2

The Beauty of Fall

Fall is a time of brilliant colors, crisp evenings, and bright blue skies. It is also a time of reflection and inspiration. Here is what some Boys Town High School students had to say about autumn's inspiration:

The beauty of fall inspires me to reach my goals by strengthening my relationship with God. When I look at all the colors of the trees and the way the sun shines, it just makes me thank God for letting me live another day to see His new creation.

—ALEKS

The air feels so much more clean and fresh. It helps you to be more open with God and the nature around you and most importantly yourself. It is important to be open minded when you are trying to reach your goals and you are not to let anything stop you or get in your way, like the birds flying south in the fall. They don't let anything stop them from getting to a better place. By reaching your goals, you are like the birds taking yourself to a better place.

– MOLLY

The fall is the most inspiring season out of the whole year for me. It is the transition of the new year. It is a time for me to get dedicated to my school work. It is the easiest time because there aren't a lot of distractions. I do not play sports and it is calm and peaceful during this time. Because of the peacefulness, this inspires me to pray more. It is a time to get closer to God. It tends to help me make wiser decisions because of the solitude.

— COLLEEN

One thing of fall is Thanksgiving and that reminds me how thankful I am to have people around me that encourage me to do my best. Another thing is that as the grass turns from green to brown, it reminds me of how I need to forget my bad things I have done in the past and to look at the bright future I have ahead of me. As the leaves are falling and turning colors it reminds me of how many times I have turned over a new leaf and how many more times I will need to turn over a new leaf.

— NICHOLE

If someone is looking for inspirations, I believe he will find them regardless of the place, season, or hour…but there are many things that occur in fall which can be seen as inspirational. Among them, I am particularly inspired by the High Holidays. I am a Jew and so these days inspire me to do better. Rosh Hashanah is the Jewish New Year. The past year and the coming new year are celebrated. Yom Kippur is the day Jews believe their fates for the coming year are entered into the Book of Life and sealed. On Rosh Hashanah, I reflect upon the past year and some of the decisions I could have made more wisely. I promise to do better. On Yom Kippur, I pray that my sins have been forgiven and that I have a better year.

— DAVIDA

🍁

Fall inspires me to reach my goals because it is like a new beginning and for us to start all over. It is a time for me also to think about God and for me to ask Him how and what I can do. It is a time for me to think about myself and to work on my treatment plan so that I can get better and be a better role model for the younger and new kids on campus.

— ALEXA

The fall makes me want to change because fall is when the leaves fall off the tree. In the fall the leaves fall off the tree like I want my past behaviors to. In the fall you can start working on your goals so in spring you can bloom like the trees do.

— BOBBI

One way the fall season helps me reach my goals is the peacefulness. I like to go outside on walks and just see nature, and just think. Fall is the prettiest time of the year, in my opinion. I think of how everything starts to die off and then I think that this is a time for me to "bloom." What I mean by this is I get a chance to start over and prove myself in school, because the fall season is when school starts. School is very important to me.

— BONNIE

To me, autumn is one of the most beautiful seasons. It is full of many changes. It is a time when everything sheds its old skin and waits for the new and better things that wait for all of us in the future. I think that the fall is one of the best times to try and reach our goals and dreams. It is a time when everything must change for the winter and wait out the tough times. This is why it is such a good idea to clean ourselves of our bad habits now. I am here at Boys Town because I need to change my bad habits. Now is the perfect time to do so.

— ROXANNE

CHAPTER 3

Cooking a Turkey

Thanksgiving dinner is the central event of the holiday, a time for fellowship and focusing on our blessings. What would Thanksgiving be without a juicy, steaming turkey with all the trimmings? Our students at Wegner Middle School offer the

following tips for preparing and
serving your turkey dinner:

1. *Go to the grocery store and pick
   out two frozen turkeys.*

2. *Then pay for the frozen turkeys.
   You don't want to eat stolen turkeys
   on Thanksgiving Day.*

3. *When they are done cooking, you
   take them out of the oven.*

4. *Then you turn off the oven so you
   don't start a fire.*

— JOHNI

1. *Put it in a steam room – 25 minutes tops.*

2. *Put leaves on the top of the turkey to keep it moist.*

3. *Give it a little TLC.*

4. *Get a baking pan out.*

5. *Put Valvoline in the pan, or butter.*

6. *Cook him for two hours, tops.*

7. *Take him out and serve him to Father Peter and everyone at Boys Town. Have a great Thanksgiving.*

– MILA

The way I would cook a turkey is, first, go to a farm and chase one. After the turkey and me ran for a long time, we would both be tired and thirsty. The turkey would go and get a drink, and while it was doing so, I would creep up closer and closer behind it. I would then get a rock and hit him with it to make him a little calmer.

I would bring it home, and when it was stuffed, I would put it in a big hole that I had dug with a shovel and had filled with coals and a hot fire. That is how I would bake my turkey. Everyone would sit down at table and say their Thanksgiving prayers, and we would be ready to eat.

— ZENIA

When you ask for the recipe for a turkey and gravy, to me that is like asking what is the most important thing about Thanksgiving and what is the least important thing about a Thanksgiving dinner. To me the most important thing is showing how much you love and care about each other. A turkey is the most important thing to eat, but your heart is what makes it special.

When you ask for the recipe for gravy, as I said before, that is like asking what is the least important thing at a Thanksgiving dinner. To me the least important thing is the food. The reason that I say the food is because if you didn't have the people with the loving hearts then you wouldn't have it. So in order to have your turkey you need some warm hearts and hands first. That is my turkey and gravy recipe.

— DOROTHEA

I would put a lot of spices on the turkey, and then deep-fry it. It's best that way.

— ANDI

Stuffing Ingredients:

> *3 bags of chips*
>
> *1 onion*
>
> *some warm water*
>
> *7 slices of bread*

Method:

> *Chop the onion up in pieces.*
>
> *Cube the bread up.*
>
> *Put the water in a glass.*
>
> *Mix it all together in a pan.*
>
> *Cook it for an hour on*
> *200 degrees.*

— JAMES

There are a lot of ways of cooking a turkey. But the best way is to do it with care. When you care about what you are doing, you will almost always do it better.

When you cook a turkey, you should be thankful you even have a turkey. You should feel very fortunate, because some people in the world cannot afford such luxuries.

We should remember that Thanksgiving is about giving thanks, and not about being a glutton. On that day, we should pray in thanks to the Lord and think about all those who are without a turkey.

It is not really hard to cook a turkey. You put it in a pan and cook it. When you pull it out, it becomes ten times better than before you cooked it.

Cooking a turkey is a lot like growing up. When it starts, it's a good thing. But as you get older, you experience more things, and life gets better and better.

The end.

— KIM

I don't know exactly how to make gravy but I'll try my best to explain it my best from what I know. The first thing you should probably do is preheat the oven, usually at about 375 degrees and then cook your turkey for 35 minutes. After you have done that take the juice from the turkey and pour it into the pan that you plan on using to cook your gravy. Next you should add some flour, usually the amount varies from 5 to 10 pounds and then you can also add a lot of water. Cook on medium high heat and stir every once in a while. Some people like to add onions but I'll leave that up to you to decide what you like to add to your gravy.

— JON

1. *First you get a turkey.*

2. *Then you take it home.*

3. *You put some water into the pan.*

4. *You have to bake your turkey at 799 degrees. It will taste very good.*

            — ERICA

I would stuff the turkey full with stuffing and put in garlic, carrots, tomatoes, potatoes, and apples for flavor. Then I would cook it at 500 degrees (so it would cook faster). Then I would take it out and we would all eat it.

            — DUSTIN

The point of Thanksgiving isn't just turkey. It's a time to thank.

— BEAU

🍁

Well, before we even take one more step, get the radio and put some music on. Then get your rhythm going and get into the groove, because that is the main ingredient of my no fail stuffing. So, let's make the food now. You feel that rhythm yet? Okay, let's start taking a half a cup of tenderness and love. Mix these all around, while shaking it all about. Make sure there's enough to go around! Then you take a gallon of happiness and blend these all together. Then throw it all into one big, loving turkey and put it in the oven

*and cook tenderly. Once your home
and heart are filled with the true
meaning of Thanksgiving, you'll know
your turkey and stuffing are finished.
Take the turkey out and bring it to the
table. What do you have? The Rhythm
and Blues Stuffing.*

— BROCK

*I don't really know how to cook
but I do know how to get the best food
in the world. The best way to eat turkey
and gravy is to get in the car, drive
down to the other side of the town
and go to the south side to my
grandmother's.*

— ANTHONY

1. *Clean turkey and find a pot.*
2. *Three-and-a-half cups of water.*
3. *One whole pan of turkey.*
4. *Add one-fourth cup of salt or other spices.*
5. *Add some good food coloring*
6. *Put it in the oven for 20 minutes and bake at 350 degrees*
7. *Take it out and cut so everyone in your family gets some. Enjoy your meal, and have a Happy Thanksgiving.*

— ADELA

First off to make gravy you need to heat the stove up. Then put the pot on the stove. Put boiling milk in. You put in seasoning and salt. You also need some cinnamon with some Dr. Pepper to make it brown. Then you put some vanilla in it with a little bit of love and some patience. Also you need some smashed potatoes with a little bit of cheese. Also a teaspoon of oats and a little bit of courage.

— ROBERT

First you tell your kids to settle down and get in the car. Then you go to Baker's and get the biggest, fattest turkey on the shelf. Next, you go home and put your kids down for a nap so they're out of the way. Then you clean the turkey. After that you whip up some of your mother's famous stuffing. If you forgot the stuffing, round your lovely kids up again and go to your mother's house and pick up the Stove Top Stuffing. After that, get your kids together and drive like a wild woman back home. Believe me, it will get you home faster. Sit down and rest for a minute. Now it's 2 o'clock and your turkey is frozen, and your parents are coming at 4 o'clock. The best way to unthaw a turkey is to throw it in the dryer for about 40 minutes on permanent press. When it's done, get out a pan and put four cups of water in it and a half stick of butter, and finally the Stove Top. Stuff the turkey with the rest of your mother's famous stuffing. Turn the crock pot on to 450 degrees, put the timer on for 60 minutes, or you can wait until it's golden brown. In the meantime, you can start the rest of your dinner – the potatoes, corn, and last, but not least, the best of all – your grandmother's pumpkin pie. Then all you have to do is check on the turkey and you are set. Wake up your kids and get them set, and make them look nice.

— AMBER

I would take the turkey and put him in a good lawn mower, and turn it on so you could take his feathers off. That's the easiest way to do it.

— JOSÉ

CHAPTER 4

A Thanksgiving Day Prayer

Lord,

We humbly ask Thy blessing
on the turkey and the dressing,
on the yams and cranberry jelly,
and the pickles from the deli.

Bless the apple pie and tea,
bless each and every calorie.
Let us enjoy Thanksgiving dinner.
Tomorrow we can all get thinner.

33

For all Thy help along the way
we're thankful this Thanksgiving day.
We're thankful too, for all our dear ones,
for all the far away and near ones.

Although we may be far apart,
we're together in my heart.
Keep us in Thy loving care,
This is my Thanksgiving prayer.

*P.S.   Anyone who wishes may help
with the dishes.*

— AUTHOR UNKNOWN

CHAPTER 5

Appreciating Autumn

Do you have a favorite fall memory? Eating crunchy apples right off the tree? Huddling with family and friends around a bonfire? Cheering on your team at a football game? Harvesting corn? We asked the students at Boys Town what the

season means to them. This is what
they said:

🍁

*The fall is a time to collect candy,
not bad memories. Go to Vala's
Pumpkin Patch and have a little fun.
Carve the pumpkins really neatly.
Don't forget to bake the pumpkin seeds.
They're too good to throw away.*

— RAQUEL

I love October. You can hear the crunch of dry leaves. Children are laughing and smiling as they go to pumpkin patches to pick bright orange pumpkins. Sometimes you can see the reflection of pumpkins in their glistening eyes. The whistling of the tearful trees and the dry cornstalks are awesome. How I love October. That warm feeling that you get when you go home to a loving and caring place and have a nice cup of hot chocolate and that snuggle you feel when you ease into your favorite chair.

– LANCE

Falling leaves are all scattered into great pieces of art. It's getting closer to winter. It's beginning to rain once in a while. There are fewer leaves on the trees. I keep on raking and jumping in the big piles of leaves. October is having fun – to the very end of the world and to the beginning of heaven on earth. This good earth is what God has made for us human beings. The falling leaves are talking to each other just like angels talk to each other. How I love October.

— KRISTI

It is fun to rake up a big pile of leaves and jump in them. I like to bag them up. These are fun things to do in October.

— CYRIL

Sometimes we don't realize that heaven is on earth because we don't pay too much attention to it. We are too busy watching TV, worried about bad weather that is about to arrive. We don't take time to go outside and look at that heaven on earth that is here. The most beautiful thing about October is the first frost. It looks so peaceful and so heaven like.

— FRED

In our younger years we are full of energy and life. But it's not 'til we age and lose some of that life that we show our true beauty and who we are inside. It is like beauty itself. For beauty takes time to develop. When beauty is finally there, it wilts quickly like the loss of a dream in the morning. It seems that we never have time to admire beauty before it fades. And the same is true in October. For it too quickly becomes November. We will always have the memories of beauty and October will come again.

— MATT

There is lots of beauty in October but the thing that is most beautiful is basketball.

— MAURICE

The one thing is the beauty of my mom. The reason I say this is because I think her sense of humor is very beautiful, not just in the month of October, but all during the year and all during her life. That makes it very fun for a person to be around her.

— AARON

*I like the color of the leaves. Even
the squirrels like the color of the leaves.*

— KAYLA

🍁

*Can't you hear the flowers
whisper to the bees?*

*Mister sun is coming out
and oh, how he sees.*

*Trees with pretty leaves,
all a work of God.*

*Red, yellow, and gold as
shiny as my mother's bowl.*

Then the snow flows down on my face.

I turn around and see
a leaf without any trace.

You can't buy friendship;
you can't buy love.

It's a gift from up above.

And if you're lucky, and if you're true

Then maybe love will come to you.

— CARLOS

Beauty is not about me and you.
It is about the leaves, flowers, trees,
animals, and the changes in the
season.

— JODY

*Fall is a wonderful time of year.
It's the time that your eyes are dazzled
by the various colors on the trees,
bushes, and the leaves that have fallen
from the trees. Everywhere you look,
you see reds, browns, yellows and some
greens. It's almost mystical how
beautiful the landscapes are. At night,
I like to watch the sun set. It is the most
beautiful thing you will ever see. The
sun lays on the ground far away and
lightens the ground in front of you. It is
really, truly amazing.*

— BRYCE

CHAPTER 6

Time for Giving Thanks

Let's look at people who are spontaneously grateful. They will give us all kinds of hints about how to help both our children and ourselves develop a sense of gratitude. Here are five examples of situations in which people are spontaneously grateful:

1. Sickness and health

A person who has been really, really sick for some time and now is restored to health is spontaneously grateful. Being sick is no fun. Being sick and in the hospital is even less fun. Most people don't know how valuable health is until they find it diminished. You don't have to actually lose your health, however, to have a sense of gratitude. One way to develop that gratitude is to visit the sick. Say to yourself, "There but for the grace of God go I."

2. Loss and gain

A person who has lost an important job or has been out of work for some time suffers a great deal, and when he or she finds an equal or better job, the sense of gratitude is almost overwhelming. It feels so good to be back at work. It feels so satisfying to be able to pay bills and know there is money in the bank. But you don't have to lose your job to be grateful. All you have to do is reflect on what a good job you have already and how fortunate you are for it.

3. Death of a loved one

Most of us have experienced the death of someone close to us, someone whom we have loved very much. We have felt the pain. We have experienced the loss. It is a pain that does not go away in a day or a week or a month. It is a loss that goes on and on.

We feel spontaneously grateful when finally we start to "get over" the loss. Happiness comes back into our lives. The morning sun seems more cheerful. The birds are happier. The squirrels are more playful; the flowers are more beautiful, and the cup of morning coffee tastes even better than before.

We are spontaneously grateful because we are much more sensitive now to life. We know how to love better and to show more care. There is a spontaneous gratitude that wells up in our hearts.

4. Something accomplished

If a person works hard – let's say working during the day, going to law school at night – and graduates, there is an enormous sense of accomplishment, and a spontaneous sense of gratitude. Or maybe someone who never learned to read has now accomplished this difficult task as an adult. There is a spontaneous sense of gratitude there as well. An immigrant to this country studies for the citizenship exam, passes it with flying colors, and is sworn in as a real American. What a sense of gratitude he or she feels!

There wouldn't be much gratitude if a law degree or citizenship were

served up on a silver platter. Think of
all the kids who never work hard but
who are passed from year to year.
They graduate from high school
without any sense of accomplishment.
But when there is real struggle,
including up days, down days, and
then a solid finish, there is a natural
and spontaneous wellspring of
thankfulness.

5. Faith in God

If you didn't have faith in God as
the good Creator of us all, it would be
very difficult to be grateful. If there
weren't a good and provident God
who loves us and cares for us and
gives us the strength to overcome

difficult times, then why would we be grateful when we survive tragedies? Winter turning into spring and spring into summer should inspire trust in God. Summer turning to fall and fall to winter should inspire me to "fall on my knees with my face to the rising sun." Beauty and splendor surrounds us.

So, to develop the spirit of gratitude, we need to help our faith grow and flourish in every way possible. We can do this through prayer and by helping others. Start the day with a reflection of these five opportunities to be thankful, and you will be surprisingly pleased with an overflowing sense of gratitude.

CHAPTER 7

'I am Grateful'

At Thanksgiving, Boys Town boys and girls have an opportunity to reflect on their many blessings. Our children come from backgrounds with more troubles than you could imagine. But simply focusing on our troubles does not make us better. Focusing on our blessings gives us a heart that begins to be filled with gratitude and joy.

I am grateful for being able to wake up in the morning. If I did not wake up, I would not be able to experience God's love and His creation today, and I could not go to my foster parents and say good morning and give them a big hug.

— NICK

I never showed gratitude when I was at home because I never felt that it was necessary. Now that I am at Boys Town, the Family-Teachers and Assistants have shown me a lot. They taught me the importance of being thankful, having gratitude, and they definitely are showing me how to get better. They told me that if I show gratitude and be respectful towards other people, getting better will just follow along. That is why I think gratitude will definitely help you get better.

— CHARLES

I am thankful for the girls in my home. They have showed me how to love. They let me know I wasn't alone. They let me know that I do have people who really care about me and are not going to let me go. The girls at my home didn't throw me away or give up when I did wrong, they just loved me more. I have learned not to push them away but to grow closer like a family I never got to have. I am grateful.

— Margaret

Boys Town has taught me that running away from your problems does not solve anything and it brings you another problem. Being here has taught me to be proud of my heritage and not be afraid of letting people know I'm Indian. Thank you for loving me and teaching me and caring about me.

— MADELINE

One thing that I am grateful for is having a second chance at life by getting to come to Boys Town and starting my life over again. I have gotten a chance here to make a future for myself and to enjoy my life. Because of all the things I have done, I would have never thought I could get a chance to come to a place as free and beautiful as Boys Town.

— JAMAR

One big thing that I am grateful for is that I am safe. I am somewhere I know people can't come in and harm me.

— TERRENCE

I am thankful for your helping me let my heart come out and shine. I'm especially thankful that when I have problems, I know that I can talk them through and that God will carry me and light a candle in my heart.

— JASON

When my parents divorced, I blamed myself a lot. After all, I had gotten bad grades in school. Maybe if I would have done better in school or at home, they would not have fought so much. That is what I believed, and I was very unhappy until I came to Boys Town and you taught me that I am not responsible for my parents' behavior. I am in charge of my own feelings, and I can make those feelings better by reaching out and by asking for help. I am grateful.

— JOHN

I am grateful for being able to wake up to pleasant people in the morning in my house. The mornings have always seemed to be the time when people are most considerate toward each other in my house. In the past I haven't always been the most pleasant to be around when I wake up. I am very grateful.

— HARLEN

The thing that I have the most gratitude for is Boys Town. Before coming to Boys Town my life was a total mess. I was breaking the rules. I was upsetting the lives of my family and friends. Hanging around me was no longer fun. In other words, I was ruining my life and starting to destroy others that I cared about.

— CHRISTINE

When I came to Boys Town, it was like I was in a prison inside myself. I did not like myself. I tried to hurt myself over and over. I was afraid, ashamed, and I kept running from my problems. Thank goodness you stopped me and held me and gave me hope. Thank you.

— MIKE

CHAPTER 8

Fostering a Sense of Gratitude

A child who gets whatever he wants whenever he wants it will never develop a sense of gratitude. During the terrible twos, a child makes huge demands. If you give in to those demands, you will have an ungrateful child. Another name for an ungrateful child is a spoiled brat.

Let's look at the dynamics of this: Let's say you and your daughter are in the grocery store at the checkout counter. Your daughter spies the M&Ms and says, "Mommy, I want one of those."

You say, "No, Maria, we can't have candy right now." What does Maria do? She escalates the request, louder this time.

What do you do? You say again, "No, we can't have those," in a louder or firmer tone. Her response is to get even louder and more demanding than she was before. This continues until she is screaming at the top of her lungs, and you finally give her the candy just to keep her quiet.

What has your daughter learned from this experience? She has learned that if at first you don't succeed, holler louder and louder until you do. What a lesson!

Is your daughter grateful when she gets out to the car with her M&Ms? Of course not. Does she say, "Thanks, Mom, for being so generous"? Of course not. An overindulged child is not a grateful child.

A grateful child is a child who knows how to accept "no" for an answer. There are three steps in accepting "no" for an answer:

- The child looks at you.
- The child says "okay."

- The child does not whine or complain.

That sounds like three fairly easy steps. But it is not so easy for a child to learn them, especially a child who is already overindulged. It takes lots of practice.

One of the most important jobs of a parent is to help a child accept "no" for an answer on a regular basis. This is one of the things a child needs to learn in order to be grateful.

Overindulging a child is an uncaring, unloving thing for a parent to do. Parents need to learn to say "no" to their own need to be liked by their son or daughter every day, all day.

To be successful at helping a child accept "no" for an answer, three things are helpful:

- Surround the "no" with a sense of calm, rather than with angry storms of emotion. You can't beat your child into gratitude.

- Stick to your guns. This may be painful for a while, but it pays off. One of the ways to stick to your guns is to model taking "no" for an answer yourself. It's a great way of helping your child learn gratitude.

- When your child does accept "no," express your approval warmly and in a heartfelt manner, not just once, but repeatedly.

There is a middle ground between overindulgence and breaking a child's spirit. It is that middle ground that is so fertile for developing a sense of gratitude. Frequently express your own gratitude in the presence of your child: gratitude for a beautiful morning, a good cup of coffee, a break in the bad weather, a bonus at work, a fun outing. It's the little things of life that are most important. Many kids haven't learned that yet, but mature people know it.

- Set some time aside at the supper table every night for each to take turns telling of something good that happened today. Make sure it is concrete

("I got an A on a spelling test"),
not abstract ("I didn't get into
trouble at school today"). Be
patient. Be persistent. Make
sure everyone takes part. At
the end, be sure to express
your own thanks and gratitude
for so many good things
happening in the life of
your family.

- Insist that your kids learn to
  say "thank you" for a good
  dinner, a rental video, or
  anything else positive. There
  are two ways of being grateful,
  and we need to teach both to
  our children. The first is to say
  "thank you" because we are
  truly happy with what was just

given us – a gift that we really wanted or something that we really enjoyed. The second is to learn to say "thank you" for things that are given to us with good intentions, even if they aren't "what we always wanted." How often do you see kids at Christmas or at birthdays tearing a gift open, not finding it to their liking, and casting it aside? That is a great teaching moment: "Joey, by setting aside your grandma's gift, you made her feel bad. Her heart was in the right place. She tried to get you something you would like. She didn't succeed, but look at how

good her intentions were. Can't
you thank her for having a
big heart?"

- Make sure you catch your kids
  in the act of giving to one
  another. Praise them for it.
  Giving is a sure sign of
  gratitude and a grateful heart.
  Even sharing candy is a sign of
  a grateful heart.

- Prayers before and after meals
  are a marvelous way to express
  gratitude.

- Finally, don't ever let a Sunday
  go by without your kids putting
  something in the collection
  plate. "What return shall I give
  to the Lord for all He has given
  to me?"

CHAPTER 9

'What I'm Thankful For'

A grateful person is an attractive person. People like a grateful person. You just like to have him or her around.

Focusing on what we have rather than what we don't have builds a positive outlook. As we help our Boys Town children learn to count their blessings, we offer them opportunities to reflect on their own circumstances and come up with examples of what makes them grateful. Here are some of their responses to the question, "What are you grateful for?"

Friends. They are there for me to help me.

— TAMMY

Prayer. It helps me focus on God.

— ROGER

Waking up and being at a safe place. I can sleep well at night and not be afraid.

— ALAIN

My mom. Because I know someone loves me.

— MANNY

Snacks. Especially when I make my privileges.

— GABBY

Love. Because not everyone in Iowa has someone to love them.

— TANIA

Stealing nothing. I used to steal cigarettes.

— GARRETT

The Nebraska Cornhuskers. But I like the Michigan Wolverines better.

— LOUIS

🍁

My Boys Town home. I don't have to live in a car on the street anymore.

— FELICIA

🍁

Eating cereal for breakfast. I like cereal a lot.

— SCOTT

Boys Town taking me in. I was unsafe before and now I am safe.

— MARTIN

🍁

The homework that I have every day. Without homework I would not be a smart and intelligent person that my teachers try to make me.

— DEVON

Having food to eat. Food can taste good or not so good, but you should eat whatever food is served because there isn't anything else to eat but food. I like it a lot.

— MICHAEL

When my dad and I went to Minneapolis and we went to a big museum and we stayed in a hotel. God let me have a good dad to do stuff with.

— TRINA

CHAPTER 10

Time to Mend Fences

According to St. Paul, the most characteristic attitude or virtue of a person in right relationship with himself, his neighbor, and God is generosity. St. Augustine said it is humility. And Martin Luther said it is gratitude.

When you think of it, they're all talking about the same thing. People whose lives are in order – with themselves, their neighbors, and their Lord – are grateful people, humble people, and generous people. It is this three-fold spirit that we at Boys Town try to encourage our boys and girls to acquire.

If you start to feel good about yourself, you tend to become more generous, more caring, more sharing, more thankful, and less arrogant.

In this Thanksgiving season, take time to mend fences with at least one person in your life – perhaps a friend or even a family member. That is the first step toward a good holiday.

Take time to mend a heavenly fence or two also. The Lord is never outdone in generosity. You probably have seen that famous "Footprints in the Sand" photo of only one person walking on the seashore with two sets of footprints. Yes, the Lord does walk by our side. But we won't notice it unless we take the Lord's hand. And walking side-by-side won't do us any good unless we walk hand-in-hand.

It is at that moment that gratitude and thanksgiving well up in our hearts. Let's share it.

CHAPTER 11

Thanksgiving
Reflections

Focusing on our blessings instead of our troubles gives us a heart that begins to be filled with gratitude and joy, and that is the road to healing and hope. These reflections of gratitude are the steps in the students' journey toward healing.

I am grateful for my Boys Town family. They have raised me. They have taught me right from wrong. They have tried to keep me safe from harm, keep me warm when I was cold, and comfort me when I needed it most.

— JIMMY

I am grateful for being able to get up in the morning and to see the light of day. Seeing the morning gets me going because it helps me to remember that God created this beautiful day for me and all poor people.

— JUAN

I am grateful for the ability to forgive and to forget because you can't be somebody if you don't forgive and forget.

— MARTA

I am grateful for bugs. They make the world very interesting.

— STEVEN

I am grateful for my step-dad. He is a good guy most of the time. The trouble is that I push him away sometimes because I only want my real dad in my life. I should be more grateful for him.

— ALLEN

*When I came to Boys Town I felt
like a weed. I felt as though I was
competing with everyone else to survive.
When they got too close I pushed them
away. I trusted nobody. Slowly my
walls are coming down. I am grateful.*

— DEBI

*I thought I was nothing. I was
worthless. It didn't really matter if I did
something right because it still wasn't
good enough. I was a perfectionist. I
am thankful I can now accept that I
can make mistakes and it's okay.*

— TRICIA

I have forgotten to be grateful for being able to think correctly. Some people end up in jail and on drugs because no one taught them right from wrong.

— JUSTIN

I am grateful for really being healthy with my diabetes. Some people have diabetes and they can do nothing to stop it.

— MELANIE

I am grateful for my freedom at Boys Town. I can say and do what I want without guards making sure I am in one place. I can wear whatever colors I want without being killed by a drive-by shooter.

— ROSA

I am thankful for people showing me that crying is better than locking feelings inside. I am thankful for giving life another chance.

— BEN

*I am grateful for my sister, Melody,
who lives with me at Boys Town,
because looking at her smiling face
really makes my day.*

— SHELLY

*I am grateful for my sister Shelly,
because no matter what has happened
to us or what our past is like, we
always have been there for each other.
I thank God for her every day.*

— MELODY

CHAPTER 12

An Attitude of Gratitude

Gratitude is the virtue I believe most characteristic of Christians. And it is especially true at this time of year.

"Dear Lord, you have given so much to me. I ask you give me one thing more – a grateful heart!"

Gratitude is infectious. Thankful people are like a refreshing spring of pure water while unthankful people pull us down into stagnant pools of selfishness.

Grateful people set resentments aside. Ungrateful people cherish resentments and horde them.

Grateful people always have room in their hearts for one more loving kindness. Ungrateful people have no room in their hearts.

Grateful people have a sense of belonging. Ungrateful people have a sense of loneliness. Ungrateful people pray, "Lord, give me an easy life." Grateful people pray, "Lord, give me the courage to be loving under any circumstances."

Focusing on our troubles does not make us better, nor does it make anyone better. Focusing on our blessings gives us a heart that begins to be filled with gratitude and joy, and that is the road to healing and hope. So we share these Thanksgiving reflections with you. I hope the words of our boys and girls encourage you to be thankful as well in this beautiful season.

I am grateful for being here at Boys Town with people who care about me and love me and who will not turn their backs when I have done wrong.

— JOE

I am grateful for having somewhere to sleep that is a safe place. I don't have to worry bad things will happen to me tonight.

— Eva

I am grateful for the kids in my house who are like big brothers and even the small ones too. We treat each other like family…no matter what happens.

— Ignacio

I am grateful for the love and the support I am receiving from my Family-Teachers and the girls in my house. They have shown me how to make the rules work for me and have saved my neck in the long run even though I resented, at times, their feedback.

— JEANNINE

I am grateful for my coaches because they have helped me to be disciplined, control my anger and taught me how to get along with others.

— JAY

I am grateful for the gift of poetry that God gave me. It helps me be able to express my feelings appropriately and get in touch with them positively.

— KATE

I am very grateful for my success in school because before I came here, I dropped out. Now I am glad I made the right choices. School has turned into something successful and even fun at times.

— JACK

I am grateful for waking up in the morning because when I was back home I lost a lot of sleep. I was scared to go to sleep. I would stay up all night because I was afraid something bad would happen to me. Here I am able to sleep with trust and confidence in God.

— TINA

❦

I am thankful for having a second chance at Boys Town because if it were not for my Probation Officer I don't know where I would be…either dead or in jail.

— JANE

I am grateful for being able to go to Boys Town and get away from the ghetto back in Texas because I was told there I would never live to see the age of 16. When I jumped into a gang, I saw people hurt, shot at, and mistreated.

— TOM

I used to be so intoxicated or blazed that the only beauty I saw was beauty nobody else saw. It was the images created by the drugs I was taking. The sun was too bright. It hurt my eyes. Now the sun makes me happy. My eyes are no longer blind to the true beauty all around me.

— DINA

I am grateful for three meals a day. Before Boys Town, I was on the streets. I barely ate. I did not have an eating disorder, but I was without money to buy myself food. After a person is hungry for so long, the pain can get so strong it makes you numb. That's what my hunger was like. Thank you, Boys Town.

— GINA

I am grateful for waking up this morning and not being drunk or still on drugs from the night before. If it were not for Boys Town, I would still be doing drugs, not be in school and I would not think straight.

— JENNY

I am grateful for all of the friends who have stood by me and who have had all their prayers answered by my coming here.

— JANICE

If I were not here I would still be on the streets hurting my family and my friends. I have learned a new way of life and obtained a new attitude.

          — AMY

I am grateful for the rules. Yes, for the rules. Because without rules the world would be so dangerous no one would feel safe. That is why I am grateful for rules.

          — ANNIE

Before Boys Town I never went to school. I had the all-time record of truancies in my school. One year I went only a total of five days and got into a fight with my mother almost every day. I was uncomfortable being around her. I was in and out of juvenile jail. None of them changed me for the better. If anything, it just made me worse. I stole a lot then. You name it, I stole it. I am grateful for my Family-Teachers. They have done so much for me.

— MARTHA

I am grateful for being able to come to school and go to church. If I weren't in some way forced, I would probably never go to church or school. The Lord knows what's good and He gives it to you. Thank you, Lord, for my Family-Teachers, who deserve my gratitude.

— ASHLEY

CHAPTER 13

What Fall Means to Me

Boys Town students were asked to personalize their impressions of nature's changes during autumn. What can we learn about ourselves from the manner in which the earth cycles and renews itself?

The beauty of fall is like the earth restoring itself. The leaves fall and the earth takes them and makes something beautiful out of them. Some people think that the fall is simply looking at leaves and raking them and throwing them away. But that's like saying to God, "Leave me. I don't want your help. I don't want to change."

— MANUEL

The fall smells way different than winter, spring or summer. I like it.

— GREG

One reason the beauty of fall is important to me is because it reminds me of my father. My father and I used to walk down the roads and pick up leaves that had fallen off the trees. They were very beautiful. Later, my father and I would do things with the leaves such as make collages and make printings on paper. I still have these things. They make me think of the fun of the falls in the past.

— JACOB

🍁

We can all admire God's artwork in the fall.

— ADDIE

*These slow, gradual changes
remind me that I too can make
changes in my life through hard work.*

— JAROD

🍁

*The beauty of fall is important to
me because it helps me get back on
track. Fall helps me to keep my mind
on today instead of being overwhelmed
with tomorrow. Fall represents change.
It shows we can all change. It shows we
can survive even through cold and
hard winter. That is why fall is
important to me.*

— CANDACE

*In the fall I like to eat grilled
cheese sandwiches and soup that
warms me up.*

— DYLAN

*One reason the beauty of the fall is
important to me is that God loves us so
much that He shows us all of His colors.
He creates a rainbow in the trees as a
reminder that He is always near.*

— JESSE

*All of these wonderful things are
silent messages from God that make
our world more special.*

— JOSEPH

To me fall symbolizes a time of forgiveness. When a tree loses its leaves, it's like our sins leaving our hearts as we ask the forgiveness of the Lord. When I see the bare trees, I think of Adam and Eve before sin. They were not embarrassed by their nakedness. I feel in the fall we don't have to hide from God. We can admit that we are sinners and that we aren't perfect. We can also ask His forgiveness and ask for another chance. Too many people overlook the beauty of the fall all too often. If we could all just take 30 seconds out of our day to watch a leaf fall to the ground and thank God for all the beauty in our lives, we just might have a happier day.

— TWYLA

The fall is important to me because football season is here and you get to drink hot chocolate at football games.

— RICHARD

The leaves make me smile if I am having a bad day at school. If I can find a really beautiful leaf, I keep it. God made the beauty of the fall and I love God more than anything in the world.

— DANIEL

I like the card sent from God that says it's fall.

— JARON

🍁

Leaves are falling off the trees. The flowers are dying. The birds are flying south. The squirrels are collecting food to store for winter. They are all like life dying and waiting to be reborn. It is like Jesus who died and rose from the dead.

— ALI

The beauty of fall is important because it is a time of year when crops are harvested. This reminds us God has provided again for us. It reminds me to be thankful.

— KEVIN

Fall is a beautiful sight to see, especially when you're sad. A fall day can brighten you up because of its beauty.

— MARCUS

I love the way the wind plays among the trees and rustles the leaves on the ground. I love the way the leaves play hide and seek on the branches of the trees. I love the soft sound of the wings of ducks and geese flapping as they fly south for the winter. I love the way pumpkins grow and the way nights darken early. I love the way the air grows colder and tickles me all over. I love the gentle sound of leaves crunching beneath my feet. I love autumn.

— Pam

When I walk through the beautiful fall leaves, I start reminiscing about past fall experiences. When I see the trees, I ponder on how a tree can have such beauty. I reach into my soul and say thank you God for this beauty. It makes me want to weep, weep, weep.

— RONALD

In the fall
I like to play ball
in the hall
and in the mall.

I love to look at the trees
right now they're all losing leaves
Some of the leaves are bright,
they crunch while walking
through the night.

In the day I like to play
in the pile of leaves,
and in the pile of leaves
were lots and lots of
bumble bees.

— LORI

The thing I find beautiful about autumn is the fresh new feel of nice crunchy leaves and the smell of delicious pumpkin pie. I enjoy seeing the glistening morning dew on the fallen leaves and the chirping of birds happily soaring through the sky. I see the vividly flaming fire colored fields. And I love to be able to go out and get the morning paper with no socks on.

— STACIE

I need beauty in my life because it makes me happy. One of the things that is beautiful is when I read a book to others and when I help others out with things. I need beauty in my life because it makes me feel good inside.

– LYDIA

🍁

Far more beautiful than
any other season
Always has the best holidays
Leaves prettiest this time of year
Love the colors.

Is my favorite time of the year
Soon snow will fall

Be very afraid on Halloween night
Everyone rakes up colorful leaves
Autumn has a nip in the air
Use the beauty of fall to
make you feel good

True beauty
Is the time to bundle up
Full of vivid colors
Usually pretty changes
Locust fly away

— JEFF

It's a time to bring maybe a little kindness to your peers. See them as not a stranger, but as a real friend. Bring happiness to others and not think of ourselves first. Come together as a true Boys Town family. Goals come into view on all agendas to become what we want to become.

— VINCENT

The fall season marks the start of a new school year. It is a great opportunity for us to start over again. We can throw away the past and move on, and to start from scratch.

— RAVEN

As the season changes many fail to realize that it brings new opportunity. As we embark on this season of fall, let us all come together with a clear focus on what lies ahead in our lives. To me fall is a time of new beginning, where we let our past experiences fall away in time to prepare ourselves for spring which is the time of new growth. We must rid ourselves of all the negative things we have gone through and make room for the next steps in our life. My goals for the fall of my senior year are to stay on track with my school work and take responsibility for my actions.

— Liz

Jesus said that He is like the tree and we are the branches. "Whoever stays connected in me will bear much fruit but apart from me you can do nothing." The same happens with the fall trees. Once the leaf is off it gets dissolved into the ground. Our lives are in much the same way like this. We all have dreams and some will fall while others will succeed. The key is to never stop rejuvenating our goals and dreams – always keep growing more leaves on different branches. This is how fall's beauty inspires me to reach my goals.

— PHILIP

Fall is like playing Follow the Leader because one leaf is following the other leaf as it drops off of the tree. The reason the leaves fall and sit at the bottom of the tree is because the wind is blowing. The wind seems to be calling the leaves to follow each other. The leaves blow back and forth looking just like kids chasing one another. By the time it gets dark the leaves stop moving and wait until tomorrow to start another game. Watching the leaves in the fall is fun.

— CORY

CHAPTER 14

How to Observe Thanksgiving

Count your blessings
instead of your crosses;

Count your gains
instead of your losses.

Count your joys
instead of your woes;

Count your friends
instead of your foes.

Count your smiles
instead of your tears;

Count your courage
instead of your fears.

Count your full years
instead of your lean;

Count your kind deeds
instead of your mean.

Count your health
instead of your wealth;

Count on God
instead of yourself.

– AUTHOR UNKNOWN

CHAPTER 15

Getting Better

These last two essays sum up the philosophy that Boys Town students learn as they begin to heal: It is by accepting help with a grateful heart and then helping others that we ourselves get better.

I feel that an attitude of thankfulness is a sign of getting better. I feel this way because a lot of people think that everyone owes them something. They think that they don't need to say thank you when they do get something or when someone helps them out. More or less they figure that, well, my life is so bad that everyone needs to do stuff for me because they have made my life the way that it is. I know this to be true because I was one of those people and still tend to be that way sometimes.

— ALICIA

In my life, I have messed up a lot. I have taken advantage of my family and things we did have. Though we had it rough, we always had enough. It was never good enough for me. I always wanted to have more or better than my friends. I was very selfish and ungrateful. I started getting into a lot of trouble at school, on the streets and in my own home. My mom couldn't handle me. She didn't know what to do anymore. The more she tried, the more trouble I caused. She was sick of my rebelling and disrespect for those around me that I had picked up from the kids I was choosing to be my friends.

About three years later, God answered my mom's prayers. I was accepted into Boys Town. It was my mother's last ray of hope left for me to have a good future. She wanted me to be happy and though she knew I didn't want to be here, she had me come here anyway. I figured that it was better than ending up in some kind of lock-up facility. For the first six months, I tried to just live life and not let Boys Town help me. Then, my cousin was getting into a lot of trouble. Our grandparents tried to get him into Boys Town, but it was denied because he had too many drug problems and did not want to get better. He was only 16 years old and already choosing his deathbed. It made me stop and realize how lucky I was to be here. I started to work with the program and slowly, with a lot of guidance and help along the way, I started progressing.

God is the One who has kept me safe this far and led me to open my heart to Boys Town. I truly believe if it weren't for God, my life would have been in lots of trouble now. I thank God every day for my life and guiding me safe this far. Someday, somehow, I will thank Boys Town and my family which has helped and stuck by my side all the way through everything. It is good to let people know how thankful

you are of them before it is too late.
You must choose the right time and
way to say it, which sometimes takes a
little while.

— RENE

Book Credits

Editing: Lynn Holm
Production: Mary Steiner
Cover Design: Margie Brabec
Page Layout: Anne Hughes